The Dynamic
of the
Provisional

By the same author:

PARABLE OF COMMUNITY
Basic Texts of Taizé

LIVING TODAY FOR GOD
VIOLENT FOR PEACE

Brother Roger's journal:
FESTIVAL
STRUGGLE AND CONTEMPLATION
A LIFE WE NEVER DARED HOPE FOR
THE WONDER OF A LOVE

The Dynamic of the Provisional

(Dynamique du provisoire)

by
BROTHER ROGER OF TAIZÉ

MOWBRAY
LONDON & OXFORD

Copyright © les Presses de Taizé 1981

ISBN 0 264 66765 4

This new translation and revised edition
first published 1981
by A. R. Mowbray & Co Ltd,
Saint Thomas House, Becket Street,
Oxford, OX1 1SJ

Translated by Emily Chisholm
and the Taizé Community

Originally published in France under the title
Dynamique du provisoire 1965, 1974
and in England as *The Power of the Provisional*
by Hodder & Stoughton Ltd, 1969

Computer assisted photo-typesetting by
Elanders Ltd, Inverness, Scotland

Printed in Great Britain by
Richard Clay (The Chaucer Press) Ltd,
Bungay, Suffolk

DEDICATED TO
VIVIAN WALES

Things are moving faster today than ever before. Only by living the dynamic of the provisional can we discover how, time after time, to keep on gaining new momentum. This will leave us free to advance – and we are all the freer, the more faithful we are to what is essential.

Ecumenism can only make progress if its inner dynamic drives it to become more and more universal. How else could the ecumenical wave slowly but surely gain ground among Christians and, through them, reach all of humanity?

Unless they are visibly in communion, can Christians go on talking about love? In the eyes of those who watch the way we live, the very credibility of the People of God is at stake.

Contents

TOWARDS A WIDER ECUMENISM

Towards a Wider Ecumenism

ECUMENISM IS STILL LIMITED

At present, a wave of ecumenism is arousing tremendous hopes. What can be done to ensure that this wave not only does not retreat, but gains ground little by little?

It is more urgent than ever that we use all our resources to give ecumenism a new dimension.

Ecumenism is the attempt to make visible a brotherly communion among Christians and, through them, among all people.

This is an extremely delicate mission, calling upon the resources of the whole personality and for a refusal to be satisfied with only partial involvement.

Ecumenism was born in the Western world, in a small number of groups who tried to awaken the Christian conscience in the face of a situation intolerable to anyone professing love for his neighbour. Coloured by its Western origins, it has remained limited instead of attaining to the universality inherent in its nature. In particular, it has not brought us much closer to Christians of the Southern hemisphere.

It came into being, moreover, in a pluralistic society where the influence of Christians, already limited, was still further diminished by their divisions.

When the incoming tide of ecumenism is channelled by Church leaders exclusively for their own purposes, it loses its power to move the younger generations, who are more and more apprehensive of anything which bears the stamp of an institution. Of course this can lead to a kind of peaceful coexistence, which in itself is a boon. But mere coexistence means coming to a standstill. Good relations, necessary as they are, are not enough.

How many Church leaders envisage only an eschatological ecumenism—for the life to come—as if visible communion were not meant to be realized on our earth. As soon as a compelling sense of urgency is lost, we prolong indefinitely a situation in which everyone is satisfied just with being listened to by the others.

Dialogue is indispensable, but it must not settle into a static benevolence between the confessions.

The tremendous hopes aroused come up against the temptation to dwell endlessly on denominational differences in all their shapes and forms. This kind of confessionalism is an attitude of self – defence. In the past it could be justified, but today those who profess it are condemned to remaining enclosed in their own shells. Besides, denominational mentalities persist even when faith has disappeared. We all know Catholics or Protestants who profess only a vague deism, but still cling to their prejudices against other Christians.

There is one force capable of making us go beyond our confessional positions. It arises when we allow ourselves to be challenged by the millions of persons who are baptised but who have no attachment to God, and by the multitudes who are totally indifferent to the faith.

Certainly it is within ourselves that all communication and dialogue find their strongest resistance. Being open to all means overcoming our self – centredness and allowing that Other than ourselves to penetrate the depths of our personalities.

14

GESTURES TO BRING US OUT OF OURSELVES

In these days paths of hope are opening up. With all the prophecies of doom that we hear, it is important to remember that very often, in the most difficult periods of history, a small number of women and men throughout the world were able to turn the course of historical developments, because they hoped against all hope. What was doomed to disintegration entered instead into the current of a new dynamism.

In order for us to advance towards a communion, God has given us the means of bringing us out of ourselves. Through the momentous events of this century, we are offered a way of emerging from the process of regression which for several centuries has been affecting Christians so deeply.

There are three gestures, in particular, which are capable of being signs of God at work, paths of communion and ways of discovering new dimensions of ecumenism:

> *Avoid separating the generations;*
> *Go to meet those who cannot believe;*
> *Stand alongside the exploited.*

Of course some decisions will always set father against son, and Christian against Christian. There will always be separations; there will always be fanatical defenders of their own selves.

But if only all those willing to participate in a common march forward would join together now! And if only Christians already together would simply refrain from passing judgement on those who travel by other roads! It is essential to credit everyone with good intentions, even those who are desperately defending bygone attitudes.

AT THE SOURCES OF THE CONTEMPLATIVE LIFE

Inspired by its generosity, the younger generation is eager to go out and encounter modern life in all its diversity. To get in touch with modern man they want to free themselves from the stock phrases and the vocabulary of the past.

We are emerging from a long period in which formulations, symbols and signs in Christian life and prayer have not been easy to understand. The desire to make a clean sweep and find other ways of drawing near to God is a healthy reaction against all mechanical repetition, lack of participation, and stereotyped expressions.

Today we are nearing a new dawn, but in its light we can perceive that relationship with God does not do away with mystery. On the contrary, there is always a line which no one can cross and beyond which the mystery remains.

When we want to make everything clear, we run the risk of understanding nothing at all, so true it is that our intelligence alone cannot grasp the mystery of God. To enter into it, nothing is more indispensable than actions, gestures, and humble signs which express the depths of the personality, the 'archetypes,' as some would say today.

Fervour cannot be nourished on explanation alone. In our life of common prayer, the gestures that have received every possible explanation will, by themselves alone, still not keep us from falling into routine.

By formulating everything, we risk losing the sense of God. This creates a vacuum into which flows indifference or even rejection, since revolt is always ready to come to life in each one of us. If we lose the sense of the mystery of God, we are tempted to turn to mockery and produce a caricature. A deep – seated force within us takes over, banishing every prompting of humility and preventing us from seeing the mystery of Christ and his Body, the Christian community.

For anyone who wants to be fully present in societies that are becoming more and more secularized without losing his sense of God, two guidelines are imperative. By means of them he will enter ever more deeply into the sources of contemplative living:

> *Live the mystery of the People of God;*
> *Remain in contemplative waiting.*

AVOID SEPARATING THE GENERATIONS

Avoid Separating
the Generations

ACCEPT THE PRESENT

Some people were already old when they were young. Their eyes turned toward the past, recent or distant, they cannot accept the changes taking place all around them. Far from accepting, they merely put up with them; 'they sneer and shake their heads.'[1]

This holds true for all social groups. So many Christians pass an irrevocable judgement on the young and thus widen the gulf between the generations. But people who grow old with no ties to the rising generations condemn themselves to vegetating. Because of the enormous changes taking place today, more than any previous generation we need to have minds and hearts open to comprehend the important developments of our time.

It is more and more the case that what we learned in our youth nowhere near approaches the levels attained by present – day knowledge. But if we use our minds day by day, they will be constantly renewed and able to adapt to new situations.

With advancing age the mind is enriched, the judgement becomes more acute and the accumulation of experience and knowledge lends an irreplaceable perceptiveness to our reflection: nothing is so valuable as a long life of hard work.

The more a man is linked to eternity, the better he

disposes himself to live, for he knows what he is drawing near to. Growing old then means being rejuvenated by everything that comes to us through contemporary developments.

If the older generations have no right to impose themselves to the exclusion of others, neither can the young take advantage of their age. The Christian community is not a copy of civil societies; everybody has their contribution to make. The generation gap goes against the spirit of ecumenism, and each one of us risks losing everything by it: the young because they no longer benefit from the human and spiritual experience their elders have acquired; the not – so – young and the elderly because they are relegated to a situation where they have no life to live, and can only wait passively for their own deaths.

One of the generations today is the hinge between two worlds, one in which parental and historical influences predominate, and another which wants nothing to do with these. It is up to those who belong to this generation to refuse to be sacrificed. If instead they see the obligation to go forward as a challenge, they will find ways of linking the mentalities of the past with the thinking of tomorrow.

It takes everybody to make ecumenism a reality, for it means, quite simply, welcoming everybody. It allows what is most genuine in each one's aspirations to blossom into fulfilment. Lagging behind hinders ecumenism, which means joining together without ever breaking anything off.

A THIRST FOR THE REAL

As I write these pages day by day, my mind is constantly kept awake here at Taizé by dialogues with many very different young people. They all have one common denominator: an intense desire to enter the world of tomorrow by participating in a rebirth of the Christian community and of the formulations of the faith.

Any sectarianism leads to a reaction of withdrawal on the part of the young who, refusing all reference to a history which no longer has anything to say to the present, will tend more and more to set themselves up in autonomous groups. Unlike their elders, the younger generation will have nothing more to do with denominational self – justifications.

They will go where there is life. They have been educated in the disciplines of technology and are eager to turn ideas into realities, so they will not put up with the delaying tactics of aged institutions much longer. If we do not discover together new paths towards communion, many young Christians will continue to search elsewhere and turn to universalist ideologies or to spirituality without God.

Conscious of their own dynamism, these generations demand authenticity. They are afraid of an abstract ecumenism which would simply be one more idea, one more ideology. They will not stand for an ecumenism which would be just a subterfuge to mask the embarrassment of division. The hour for concrete gestures has arrived.

Among the younger generations of Christians two tendencies exist, both fired by one and the same enthusiasm. Some young people, distressed by the unwieldiness of institutions, turn their distress into aggression. They cannot see any other way out but to break the structures and destroy the old pockets of Christian institutionalism. As far as rebuilding goes, their views are sometimes only theoretical.

Other young people, taking concrete situations into account, want to introduce a new today into the community of Christians. They know that rebirth is not a game, nor does it mean calling everything into question for the sheer pleasure of getting people all stirred up—an infernal circle in which we enclose other people to satisfy our own need for change. And so they do not wish to build in the abstract, or in isolation.

It is true that the situation which must be overcome in the next decades is characterized by several centuries of marking time; at one point each of the different groups of Christians, in order to survive, had to consolidate its own traditions, even if that meant cutting themselves off from one another. Marking time hardens and leads unfailingly to disintegration: anyone who stops creating is heading for self – destruction, in the short term or in the long.

THE GOSPEL IN ITS ORIGINAL FRESHNESS

The younger generation is asking for new signs. Does the Holy Spirit only speak through mature men, the wise men that we have perhaps become? Might he not also speak to the People of God through the new generations? Will their questions succeed in touching us to the quick?

At times the young judge Church leaders harshly. They feel that adults have acquired unjustifiable securities, the privileges which go with institutions, and so they refuse to enter into communication with them.

They want the Christian community to be uncompromising. They are revolted by cleverness. They demand a new life – style and, if they do not find it, they prefer to leave the Church and go where they think they see more simplicity and more sincerity in human relationships.

What is the best that this generation has to say to us? 'Give us existential proof that you believe in God, and that your security is truly in Him. Prove to us that you are living the Gospel in all its original freshness, in a spirit of poverty, in solidarity with all and not only with the family of your particular Church.'

The Gospel in all its freshness? That means a constantly renewed waiting for God. It means living in the dynamism of the present, continually returning to the sources. It means reconciliation.

In order to recover the original freshness of the Gospel, could we accept a second conversion? The word is inapt, charged with the emotional overtones our forebears sometimes gave it. But we adults, are we afraid of renewals that are all the more difficult because habits formed over the years and human pride run contrary to the spirit of poverty and to authentic waiting? Pride creates a cleavage through which all the freshness of the Gospel trickles away. But if we accept this conversion in its totality, Christ will enter into the depths of our minds and our hearts. He will even penetrate our bodies, so that in our turn we will have 'bowels of mercy.'

CREATING TOGETHER

Whether they are Catholics or Protestants, the rising generations demand more than reforms: they demand a rebirth of the Christian community. But very often they put the cart before the horse, forgetting that there is no reform of community without reform of the individual. Being must come before doing. Obsessed by the will for reform, we run the risk of forgetting that renewal begins in the depths of ourselves.

To these young people I keep on saying: in the brotherly communion which brings together several generations today in Taizé, we want to listen to the Holy Spirit in you, enlarging our minds, our spirits and our hearts. Ask God for our conversion and we will build together, and together we will say: 'Look, Lord, upon your people; consider our brothers and sisters the world over. We have separated; we do not seem to be able to join together in a common creation. Break down our self – sufficiency. Inflame us all with the fire of your love.'

And I also say to them: nobody constructs starting from nothing. The power of the forces that inhabit you can lead you to believe that you are going to rebuild entirely on your own. But the genius of the People of God is to construct with everybody. Do not forget yesterday. Nothing enduring is accomplished unless it is created along with others.

In the common life of the People of God as in every Christian community, including marriage, each individual member plays his part day by day in re – creating the whole body. If one member is dominated by a personal creative passion, and does his work without integrating it into the creative work of the community, he destroys without realizing it.

For people really to live a common life, the aim of all must be to build together. The sign of communion which will then shine out among men is more important than the noblest piece of individual effort, worked out on the fringe of the community.

Our creative work becomes communal as soon as we consider what God is preparing for us. So many signs are given us today. God is preparing for us a Christian community which will be a place of communion, offering to the insecure throughout the world a firm base. No violence will be used to achieve this communion. No one will ever be required to renounce his own Church or his own family. That would not be creating together. To do so would be to wound love, and anyone who wounds love is not building up the People of God.

GO TO MEET THOSE WHO CANNOT BELIEVE

Go to Meet Those Who Cannot Believe

Now, at the end of the twentieth century, we Christians are confronted with the result of our divisions—mutual impoverishment.

We are surrounded by non – Christians, and also by Christians for whom the faith is a matter of indifference. They can only believe what they see with their own eyes. How can they take us seriously as long as our brotherly love is not plain for all to see?

A time of confrontation is coming. We are all concerned because we are all challenged. After twenty centuries of Christianity, more and more baptised persons are losing interest in the faith. At the same time, in spite of our Christian presence throughout the world, living conditions are deteriorating year by year in certain regions of the globe.

Our communion is a function of all these people; it is for them all. We do not desire it for our own happiness, nor to be stronger over against others. We desire it solely in order to follow our vocation to be universal. That is the aim of ecumenism; it is the first step, to make us able to offer people a place of communion for all. Is not the People of God still the only reality capable of offering a brotherly communion to people all over the world?

We will never encounter those who do not believe

unless we are all together. Not that we are asked to betray the truth! But if we agree on one basic truth, the necessity of visible communion, we will have found the existential possibility of agreeing one day on other truths of the faith.

There is the promise of a new dynamism to those who come together again after separation. Anyone who has achieved reconciliation finds that his mind and heart have been opened, and even in old age he renews his youth. Reconciled with himself and his neighbour, he regains vital energy. In the same way, Christians throughout the world will experience in the rediscovery of visible communion the youthfulness and vitality of a new springtime.

There is a dynamic of reconciliation which will bring us out of the state of impoverishment brought about by our divisions. Its impetus will allow us to overcome our inability to join a world which, though it may not expect much from us, would be justified in expecting everything from men and women who call themselves Christians.

But the confrontation now in preparation will mean, in the strongest sense of the word, an awakening for everyone. For all of us, together, to go and meet those who cannot believe, we are asked to make the secret offering of our lives day by day.

The real history of the ecumenical movement will never be written. It lies in the faithfulness in things large and small of those whose whole inner life is engaged in the struggle. For a long time to come ecumenism will be advancing against the stream of conformity; dialogue with those farthest from us will never happen as a matter of course. Anyone who is unwilling to accept this struggle should ask himself if his ecumenism is not a plant without roots.

DIALOGUE WITH EVERYONE

At Taizé the vocation to ecumenism has made us open, year in year out, to all that is human. It has awakened in us an interest in those who were farthest from us. Without a passion for the unity of the Body of Christ, we never would have discovered this friendship with so many people all over the world.

Our concern for dialogue has made us attentive to everything human. Who would not burn with desire to understand another human being in his life – struggle: the light that has gone from his eyes or the hard – won serenity, the whole personality held in check, the scars of conflicting impulses, the generous gift of himself or the firm will to keep himself back.

The spirit of mercy disposes the heart of stone to become a heart of flesh. It leads to a strong love, devoid of sentimentality, that caricature of tenderness. It refuses to turn the spotlight on oneself. It invites us to accept in quiet trust our neighbour, whoever he may be, and any event whatsoever.

Why is it that, although they say they know God, so many Christians behave as if they had never found him? They show no mercy. They profess the God of Jesus Christ and yet their hearts remain hard.

On the other hand, why is it that so many agnostics, in the wake of the publicans and tax – collectors, 'are entering the Kingdom ahead of us?' They open up a way of peace, they are men and women of communion, and they often show greater concern for peacemaking than many Christians do.

It is possible to believe that people of this kind are unconsciously bearers of Christ, although they have no explicit faith. Could this not be the result of the prayers of so many Christians throughout the ages? People hear God's voice without recognizing him; they are obedient to him and they live lives of charity. How can we avoid applying the words of Christ to them: 'They go before us into the Kingdom?'[2] They open doors for us; they clear the way.

There are many who profess to love Christ but do not know him. And there are many who love him, although they claim that they do not know him.

There are many who are children of light unawares. In any case they are easy to recognize: full of concern for their neighbours, they flee the works of darkness, all that is murky and lacking in transparence.

Dialogue with someone who does not believe sometimes allows us to discover in him what he does not recognize by himself, the mystery of a hidden presence.

A Christian who senses in his neighbour the most ecumenical qualities, who seeks in him the being God created, benefits from the mutual re – creation involved in all dialogue.

Only someone whose life is animated at all times by the Word of God and the Eucharist can speak like this, of course. Otherwise the result would be relativism, which does nobody any good. To say that there are people who follow God without knowing him could constitute an invitation to cease all combat for Christ. What then would be the good of praying, or of remaining in God's presence?

STAND ALONGSIDE THE EXPLOITED

Stand Alongside
the Exploited

THE CLASH BETWEEN TWO WORLDS

Christians are becoming more and more aware of the conditions of injustice and oppression which characterize human relationships. This realization needs to be continually brought up to date. On re – reading this chapter after nine years with a view to a new edition, I now find that what I wrote then did not go far enough. And so I have retained only a few passages.

One day an intolerable divorce will cleave the world in two, if those who live in the Northern hemisphere remain indifferent to the two thousand million whose poverty continues to increase, in the Southern hemisphere as well as in vast areas of the rich countries. If, together with them, we do not seek to advance towards the liberation of mankind from oppression of every sort, the meeting of two worlds could well turn into an ever widening rift.

An economic and cultural system worked out in the Northern hemisphere has brought the Southern continents to the state of dependency with which we are familiar. The continents of the North are met more and more by curt refusals from the Southern hemisphere. And in the Northern hemisphere many are beginning to consider their own privileges intolerable.

If only Christians were able to make Peter's words come true: 'I have neither gold nor silver,'[3] I have no capital in reserve and nothing superfluous, the course of many an historical evolution would be turned back. The struggle to set every human being free, the struggle to promote a society without classes would find a base of support. The rising generations desert us Christians who speak glibly of security in God when we often need so much insurance in gold and silver.

But today, still more is required of us. Generosity and detachment are not enough. Communion with the poverty – stricken in the world also means participating in the world's struggle against its poverty. The Christians' place is in the thick of this struggle, at the front lines, in the rich countries as well as in the poor.

THE SPIRIT OF POVERTY

Today a strong call for poverty is making itself heard among Christians. Many young people are critical of every sign of wealth. Throughout history, to this very day, so much wealth has been accumulated by Christians, and by the Churches themselves. Christians have moved further and further away from the 'socialization' which was a fact in the early Church.

Poverty is a word that scorches the lips. When I was writing the Rule of Taizé, I hardly dared use it; my pen could scarcely bring itself to write it. Thinking that the spirit of poverty lay first and foremost in simple sharing, I preferred to speak of a commitment to community of goods 'which might imply possible poverty.'

We may have to give up many material possessions, but the spirit of poverty goes still further. Poverty of means might lead us to seek compensations elsewhere, for example by commandeering other people, forcing them to fit into our scheme of things.

The spirit of poverty embraces the whole of our being. External signs of poverty are not enough. They do not prevent us from still cherishing a human ambition, a need for power or a desire to dominate sometimes belied by outward appearances.

Sometimes too a puritanical attitude prevails. It consists in acting poor, in other words looking drab, when wealth is hiding behind the faded exterior. 'Happy the heart that is poor.' If the spirit of poverty became synonymous with gloom and austerity, how would it correspond to the first Beatitude? The spirit of poverty is found in the joy of a man who trusts in God. It shows itself in outward signs of joy.

There are also those who advocate an ideal of poverty unattainable in an affluent society. They place those who want to be poor according to the Gospel in a state of permanent conflict: they desire to attain the inaccessible.

To ask for the impossible leads to crisis situations. Insisting too much can imprison a man in his inner conflicts. Are we not witnessing, in some circles, the establishment of a neo – Jansenism?

It is true that many men and women have taken a vow of poverty in response to a radical call. When their poverty is lived without passing judgement on others, it is joyful waiting for Christ to return, and genuine solidarity with those throughout the world who have no daily bread. It is, as well, the protest of the Christian conscience at the abuse of the earth's riches and at exploitation. The earth has been given to man for his use. It is a means of liberation, not of impairing the freedom of others.

If it is accompanied by fanaticism, a commitment to poverty is not only unedifying—the bitterness it contains is destructive. The man or woman who has taken a vow of poverty must not forget the father or mother of a family whose way of life is very different. People who are fanatically poor are frightening.

The spirit of poverty does not lead to complacency. One Beatitude cannot be exaggerated at the expense of the others. The poor are gentle; they remain Christ's poor. Without charity poverty is nothing—shadow without light.

Within the people of Israel there was a community of poor people. They lived in the presence of God, awaiting the coming of the Messiah, eager for the imminent fulfilment of the promise. The accumulation of possessions would have given the lie to their hope. In this community the Virgin Mary was ready and willing, and she was able to pronounce the yes of a faithful heart.

Today among suffering humanity throughout the world, many belong to the community of Christ's poor. Some more than others, they are eagerly living and waiting for his return. Among them can be found one of the great treasures of the Gospel, which Western Christians, enervated by the accelerating pace of developments, are losing: the awareness of God's providence. As we take part in their struggle, we do indeed discover a sense of urgency, but at the same time we learn that waiting can be dynamic. Through them we become capable of understanding what our dense minds could no longer comprehend.

Inspired by the spirit of poverty, a man learns to depend on God. We are poor in skills, poor in resources; but he is there, and he fills us to overflowing. Multiplying securities of all kinds gives the lie to our trust in God. Abandoning them means seeking God and finding unshakeable security in him alone. In the wilderness the people of Israel tried to keep the manna from heaven for the morrow, but it was already going bad.

LIVING THE MYSTERY OF
THE PEOPLE OF GOD

Living the Mystery of the People of God

SOLIDARITY WITH ALL THE BAPTISED

The ecumenical vocation leads us inevitably to reflect upon the People of God and in particular to realize that by their baptism all Christians belong to Christ and to his Body. Orthodox, Catholic, Protestant, we are all stamped with the seal of the universal by one and the same baptism, and intended to become people able to discern in every creature the image of the Creator himself.

We all confess in the same way our relationship to Christ, the Head, and to his Body, the People of God. When we declare 'I believe in ... the communion of saints,' we are affirming: I believe that between the witnesses who have left us and the Christians on earth who struggle and pray, there exists a relationship which nothing can destroy. An identical communion binds together all the baptised who are alive on earth today. Because of this common baptism by which we are all rooted in Christ, we are asked to live in solidarity with all the baptised and to remain in unshakeable fellowship.

For a Catholic, to be in solidarity with all the baptised means first of all being in solidarity with all the spiritual families which are the soul of Catholicism. At this stage of history, we expect Catholics not to reject one another. If the various tendencies which are manifest were to prevent dialogue, it would be an unparalleled setback for ecumenism.

In the midst of their disarray, may those who have a sense of the things that endure, a sense of the holy, see in the Christians opposite them men and women with an overriding concern for dialogue with those who are far from the faith. May those who have been granted a sense of the mystery of the Church refrain from keeping for themselves the irreplaceable values to which they are attached, and understand those who have a passion for dialogue with their contemporaries. And may the Catholics who are in the front lines learn once again that, without a daily return to the sources, very soon they will have nothing to offer but their own emptiness.

After an initial period of inevitable tension, we hope all the various spiritual families will discover the Gospel values each of them contains.

A Christian's life is demanding enough as it is! Why waste energy in condemning? Why wear ourselves out in despising other schools of thought? Any argument arising from blind hatred proves nothing.

How many Christians are still capable of wielding anathemas, particularly in minority situations of whatever denominational background, as if constant defensiveness were their only means of survival! In their aggressiveness such people always claim that another school of thought is not representative. But what are the people who speak like this representing? What light are they shedding in the world of today and among the People of God in its march forward?

We are very often particularly hypersensitive in what concerns our own confessional positions. Did not our fathers risk their lives to defend these very positions? Dwelling on the past history of battles and of tears paralyses our energies. Our sensitivity quickly overflows and becomes exaggerated, and then, to avoid being bruised, retreats into its shell. A refusal to brood over yesterday's wounds and today's is the only way out.

Nothing is more contrary to solidarity than a double – faced ecumenism, an ecumenism with no risks attached. Those practising it show much kindness and balanced judgement in their dialogue with Christians of another persuasion, but they criticize the others as soon as they are safely back in their own camp. In so doing they gain credit with those who are in favour of ecumenism, as long as everything stays just as it has always been.

This equivocal attitude, not to say this ecumenical 'double life,' is one of the supreme temptations. It is the prelude to future disappointments. To call oneself ecumenical, and all the time be afraid of unity, leads to impounding the ecumenical wave in the institution, stopping it from rebounding and causing it to fall back again.

In 1519, as he was commenting on the Biblical text 'help carry one another's burdens, and so you will fulfil the law of Christ,'[4] Luther seized the opportunity to say what he thought about the schism of the Hussites in Bohemia, which had taken place before the Reformation:

> 'The Bohemians who have separated from the Roman Church can indeed bring forward excuses for what they did, but these excuses are blasphemous and contrary to all Christ's commands. Their separation is in fact contrary to the love which sums up all the commandments. What they advance as their only argument is precisely the worst accusation against them: they claim that they have separated for fear of the Lord and on grounds of conscience, in order not to live among corrupt priests and popes. Even if priests or popes or anybody else were corrupt, if you were burning with true Christian love, you would not run away, you would go running towards them, from the ends of the earth if need be, to weep, to exhort, to persuade and to set everything going again.
>
> 'Know that in obedience to this teaching of the apostle ("carry one another's burdens"), what you must carry are not the pleasant things, but the burdens; which means that all the glory of those Bohemian brethren is nothing but outward show. It is the light in which the angel of Satan is disguised.
>
> 'And we, are we going to run away and separate because we have to bear the burdens and the truly intolerable monsters of the Court of Rome? Far from it! Far from it! On the

contrary, we reprimand, we are incensed, we plead, we exhort, but we do not break the unity of the Spirit, and we do not stand on our dignity. For we know that love overcomes all things, not only defective institutions, but also men who are monsters of iniquity. A love which bears only the good qualities of another is a lie.'[5]

Luther took the initiative which was to lead to division in the sixteenth century. Yet he had an acute sense of the Church, otherwise no such passage could ever have come from his pen. He was not aware of any definitive break, still less of the consequences we perceive today. What he went through, along with many others of his time, was a dilemma of conscience. Perhaps we would not be where we are today if the confrontation made possible by the Second Vatican Council had taken place in the sixteenth century. How many times during Council sessions did I call to mind the figure of Martin Luther! I used to say to myself: if that man were here in St Peter's, he could only rejoice at hearing his most fundamental aims expressed in this place, the aspirations which, initially, were closest to his heart and inspired his actions. But the clock of history cannot be turned back.

Neither was generosity lacking on the Catholic side in the sixteenth century. Some expressed genuine distress and worry. In 1522, the Diet of Nuremberg called the German princes together to decide on a common policy toward Luther and the dawning Reformation. Pope Adrian VI sent a legate to whom he had given these written instructions:

'You must say that we freely acknowledge that God has permitted this persecution because of

49

the sins of men, priests and prelates in particular. Holy Scripture teaches us throughout that the faults of the people most often have their source in the faults of the clergy. That is why, when our Lord wanted to purify the unhealthy city of Jerusalem, he first went into the temple to pray. We know that for years now, even in the Holy See, many abominations have been committed: the abuse of holy things, transgression of the commandments, so much so that everything has been turned into scandal. All of us, prelates and clergy, have forsaken the way of righteousness.'[6]

In one sense, the vocation of the Reformation was initially the determination to amend and deepen Catholicism. Protestantism, however, has sometimes set itself up in an isolation untrue to its original insights. The danger, then, is that this can lead to an attitude of simply waiting for the Catholic Church to 'become Protestant.'

In the long run positions hardened. What was a dilemma of conscience was superseded by attitudes of defensiveness or complacency on both sides. Those who did not ask for the break made the most of their being in the right, and those who brought it about believed they were on the right side of the fence – hadn't they weeded out the tares from the wheat?

Catholics and Protestants formed defensive blocs. To protect her members and to preserve them from new separations, the Catholic Church set in motion and encouraged a movement of Counter – Reformation. In many respects her thinking developed in opposition to Protestantism. On the Protestant side, confessional systems of thought were based on the negation of anything that appeared to be Catholic. Furthermore, in the course of its history Protestantism has included minorities which have had to justify their existence over against a Catholic majority. This formed habits of defensiveness so characteristic of a certain mentality.

If both sides do all they can to promote the re – births that are essential, the day will dawn when we realize that we have come together again. If renewal is put into practice by both parties, they will meet at the end of the road. The insights born of the Reformation as well as those of the Catholic tradition will be seen to complement each other and will be brought into harmony.

The most successful renewals will no doubt always leave lingering elements of sectarianism in their wake. But that should not make us lose heart.

On the Catholic side, the Second Vatican Council has opened a way forward, a way full of promise and dynamism. An event of God has burst forth, at the risk of terrifying some non – Catholics who are afraid of being engulfed in a tidal wave. But once the initial shock is over, the most alert of the non – Catholics will have taken stock of this event.

It is up to Protestants to make up their minds whether, for their part, they are going to keep on looking back to their past history or whether they, in their turn, will accept the possibility of re – birth.

After four and a half centuries we are forced to admit that a renewal in Protestantism is necessary for it to rediscover that dynamic of the provisional which should have been the reason for its existence—not to settle down so as to last forever. It is true that this renewal is not made any easier when some Catholics speak of the 'return' of their separated brethren. This expression hurts, because it suggests a retrograde movement, an unconditional surrender. Such a conception is far from the mentality of contemporary man, who tends always to move forward and to leap over obstacles. Communion among Christians will not be the triumph of some over others. If it had to be victory for some and defeat for others, nobody would accept it.

Protestants today are in danger of living under two illusions.

As heirs of a Reformation, they could think that the reforms have been made once and for all. They believed they had rediscovered the purity characteristic of the Church in its first flowering. But it is difficult for them to agree even on a common conception of the early Church, and on the point in time when this first period ended. Have not their own communities, moreover, been infected by complacency, and by the accumulation of traditions, institutions and doctrinal developments further and further removed from the original thinking of the Reformation? Their institutions are weighed down with more than four centuries of history. Who will be able to promote a new and profound rebirth, so that they can speak to contemporary man?

Another illusion would be to assume that, as a result of the reforms issuing from the Second Vatican Council, Catholicism is going to 'protestantize' itself. Would that not be fostering a 'return to the fold' mentality in no way different from that for which Protestants reproach others? As if they only had to remain as they are, and wait for the Catholics to come to them.

'God's good time' is here today. Will they be able to welcome it in simplicity of heart and humility? Are they going to retreat into new self – justifications, or will they be able to do everything possible to exhort, persuade, support and bring to fulfilment rebirths of the People of God.

It may be necessary to react to the dead weight of a Christian community. But if those who express themselves in this way become protestors and if, moreover, they regroup and clamour from without, they hold back the Christian community, exhausted as it is from its long journey, and they hinder its rebirth. How can we become leaven in the dough, to raise it up and to burst the crust which continually re – forms over ageing institutions? Nothing can resist such leaven.

Threatening to break off relations is a dangerous tactic. It is always from within and with infinite patience that what should be revived is revived. And it is only then that confrontation becomes creative. Though at the time it seems to ease tension, every break is an impoverishment in the long run. It is a refusal to move ahead and to undertake the ventures essential to every life in God that is fully responsible and in solidarity with one's neighbours.

The temptation is indeed great for some to pull back and then, with the best people, form a little Church group. But we must realize that under the pressures of history, 'tiny remnants' run the risk of fossilizing and of no longer being bearers of life. And all that does not promote life is doomed to die.

The diversity of spiritual families within the People of God makes for health and universality. But those whose particularities can only subsist at the price of separation militate against unity.

Reflecting on the mystery of the People of God, accepting our own impotence in the face of certain encumbrances, enables us at the right time to ask, to plead, to exhort and to prepare for the explosion of God's event in the midst of the Christian community, but without ever breaking the communion.

Anyone who, in his personal or his Church life, is content simply to wait for God to act and to live solely in the provisional, will soon see his waiting invalidated. If he refuses to accept that the event of God must enter into history and into the continuity of tradition, he will expose it to the danger of being like a pearl cast before swine.

But on the other hand, anyone who does not allow for the constant possibility of the event of God forgets the value of waiting, deprives himself of the dynamic of the provisional and condemns himself to fossilization and the darkening of his light. To maintain stereotyped forms in the name of tradition is to caricature the tradition itself, that great stream flowing through the ages and the life of the People of God, bearing in it and with it essential values, the living Word of God. Anyone who expects nothing new becomes static. He loses all ability to communicate.

It can happen that when God acts decisively in the Christian community there is great tension, great suffering even. Then, more than ever, contemplation of Christ and attentiveness to the mystery of the People of God come to the aid of our impatience and bring us serenity once more.

HEALING THE BREAK

The call for reconciliation and solidarity is a language meaningful to everybody. Too often those in authority are tempted to label naive the faith of men and women who, to prove that things are on the move, forge ahead and act in ways which go against the stream. It is a serious matter to caricature the way in which the humble express their faith, and to mistake a childlike spirit for childishness. To call naive or sentimental the assurance of those who, in the simplicity of their prayer, count on God for everything, is to cast doubts on the seriousness of their faith.

Here are two couples, both separated but desiring reconciliation.

The first looks backwards and does not live in God's today. Both partners want to justify themselves, to have guarantees, to teach the other a lesson. Good reasons pile up over and over again; arguments multiply. Encounter remains impossible.

The second couple has a kind of presentiment: if the family is to exist again one day, the time comes when there is no other solution but to come together under the same roof and try to live and get along together. This means they have to refuse to accuse one another, to give up once and for all their belief that separation is justified, and discover themselves and each other in a brand – new solidarity. Once the introductory dialogue is over, communion between Christians will not be accomplished without the act of faith which consists in making our solidarity visible, by living together in the same Church reality. Those who are separated and eagerly await communion realize that their situation is provisional, and this stimulates them to advance. For those who refuse to give up hope, the price to be paid for communion between Christians is this: at all times they must be able to keep going forward beyond their own limitations, in the most ecumenical setting possible.

The Eucharist, which is at one and the same time the source and the goal of unity, is alone capable of giving us the strength and the means of making communion among Christians a reality on this earth. This is a vital truth. The sacrament of communion is offered to us to dissolve all the ferments of separation in and around us. By it those who despised one another through ignorance are bound together.

The ecumenical wave will fall back if the day does not soon arrive when those members of different Churches who believe in the real presence of Christ in the Eucharist all meet around the same Table.

The ministry of authority in the People of God is often called into question. These doubts correspond to a mentality that rejects anything that stems from the previous generations.

This ministry in the People of God exists for the sole purpose of fostering communion. It is there to gather together, to unite those who are always separating, dividing and opposing. Those who have received this function are above all servants. Their pastoral task, their service, is to help the Christian community entrusted to them to move towards unanimity, that is to say, literally, to have only one soul, '*una anima.*'

Every Christian community is a microcosm, a visible image of communion. It cannot exist without a head, someone who has received the office of uniting, if need be exhorting, and above all of reminding everyone of the spirit of mercy without which no Christian community is possible. If the Church requires, at the head of each community, someone who fosters unanimity, who re – groups what always tends to disperse, should she not also accept a pastor of pastors and communities who will be tireless in keeping them all together?

And yet many refuse these ministries of communion, asserting that Church leaders, more than other men, give in to ambition. It is true that pride and vanity are pitfalls lying in wait for those holding positions of authority in the Church.

Human ambition is utterly opposed to poverty of spirit. When it slowly gains ground, it must always find new pastures. Developments in contemporary psychology often create a will to 'self – fulfilment.' How many have run after that mirage, the ambition to 'fulfil themselves!' But what does this expression mean in terms of the Gospel?

One of the great combats to be waged against oneself is

indeed the struggle for humility, and it is a virtue sorely put to the test in anyone who accepts responsibility. The slaking of pride brings temporary relief, but the craving for power returns, more and more insatiably.

Those who hold such positions in the heart of Christian communities sometimes yield to the same inner tendencies – authoritarianism, intrigue, and seeking relief from humiliating wounds in the compensations of ambition.

Non – hierarchical institutions do not protect those in charge and do not place them in a privileged position. Protestant pastors too have been known to become victims of an inhuman religious establishment. Authoritarianism creeps in everywhere, among the leaders of Protestant Churches as well. Do not some of them have precisely that thirst for power which they sometimes criticize in those belonging to a hierarchical Church?

Nowadays men entrusted with responsibilities are sometimes unable to find time for converse with God. In many cases men overburdened with duties come to give first priority to coping with their overwhelming tasks. For lack of time, they sometimes give up their dialogue with God. Their innumerable activities no longer permit them to find in God the necessary perspective on things.

An understanding of these human situations allows us to live something of the mystery of the People of God.

INSERTED INTO HISTORY

In creating a common life at Taizé, our sole desire was to be a family of brothers committed to following Christ, as an existential sign of the communion of the People of God.

A life in community is a living microcosm of the Church, an image on a small scale containing the whole reality of the People of God. And so the humble sign of a community can find a resonance far beyond the limitations of the individuals who make it up.

The world of today needs images more than ideas. No idea can be accepted unless it is clothed in visible reality, otherwise it is only ideology. However weak the sign, it takes on its full value when it is a living reality.

To live out our ecumenical vocation authentically, we must be deeply concerned to realize a communion in our life together. The fact that some of us belong to different Reformation Churches or to the Anglican Communion, and that it is possible to have Catholic brothers as well, does not in any way put up barriers between us. The communion of faith is forged through liturgical prayer, and takes shape slowly.

We know that we are not in a privileged situation, for our combat is intense. But if we had to start all over again, we would not hesitate.

With the great freedom given by our situation, we might well have taken no account of those who preceded us in the common life. But what sort of a life would that have been, lived outside of all solidarity? Being attentive to the mystery of the People of God has led us to consider that Taizé is only a simple bud grafted on a great tree, without which it could not survive.

In this regard it is undoubtedly significant that our village lies between Cluny and Citeaux.

On the one hand Cluny, the great Benedictine tradition which humanized everything it touched. Cluny, with its sense of moderation, of visible community built up in unity. Cluny, the centre of attraction for men consciously or unconsciously seeking their own inner unity and unity with their neighbours.

Among the abbots of Cluny is the figure of that outstanding Christian, Peter the Venerable, so human, so concerned for charity and for unity, capable of gestures centuries ahead of his time. So it was that when two popes had been elected by the conclave, he was magnanimous enough to ask the one who belonged to Cluny, one of his own brothers, to step down for the sake of unity.

In advance of the thinking of his time, he welcomed and offered shelter to Abelard, a man public opinion had condemned.

At that period of history it was he, once more, who inspired his contemporaries by announcing in words of fire the power of a personal encounter:

> 'Jesus will always be with me, and he will never turn away from me at any time. Certainly not at any time, for, despising and rejecting all that is not he, I will attach myself to him alone. Jesus will be my life, my food, my rest, my joy. He will be for me my country and my glory. Jesus will be everything for me: here below as far as possible, in hope and love until the gate of eternity: then I shall see him face to face. He has promised.'[7]

On the other hand there is Citeaux, revitalized in Peter the Venerable's time by another Christian no less remarkable: Saint Bernard.

Saint Bernard foreshadows all the reforming zeal which was to explode in the sixteenth century. He renewed

Citeaux to reform the Rule by which Cluny lived. He refused to compromise the absolute of the Gospel in any way. He spoke the language of a Reformer. He was more concerned with the demands of the present moment than with historical continuity. To one of his brothers he wrote:

> 'There is nothing stable in this world ... and so, of necessity, we must either go forward or go back. To remain in the state one has reached is impossible. Anyone unwilling to advance retreats. It is Jesus Christ who is the prize of the race. If you stop when he is striding on, you not only come no closer to the goal, but the goal itself retreats from you.'[8]

Fusing the sense of urgency with a sense of the continuity assured by several generations is an incomparable factor making for inner peace and humility: I am a useless servant; what I do not accomplish myself, others will accomplish after me. From what is now still immature, others will be able to gather the ripe fruit.

We are grateful to those who have gone before us for remaining consistently faithful to the call of the Gospel. We were all called to one and the same commitment to leave all, and to receive a hundredfold here on earth, together with persecutions.

By the witness of their life as brothers which has so often evoked the comment: 'See how they love one another,' by their obedience to God manifested in the humble fidelities of everyday life, by the continuity of their praise throughout the centuries, by many other qualities of life kept alive down the ages, they support us and give us grounds for hope. In some periods of history they have maintained through a great diversity of spiritual families the unity necessary for the building up of the Body of Christ. By being living signs of communion in this way, and by offering their lives day after day anew, they lead us onward in the very footsteps of Christ.

If we are told about the difficulties that weigh upon some of them, we keep silent. It is so true that judgments from outside have always led to a hardening of positions. When some of them suffer, our only wish is to love them all the more. And should the opportunity arise of expressing our own view, we do so only when we are sure of not fostering a spirit of antagonism. Otherwise we would be giving the lie to our ecumenical vocation. We would be protesters, and in that way imprison ourselves in a position of self – sufficiency. Implicit in our very existence would be a judgment no less severe for being unexpressed. Communion cannot come about through protest. Our readiness to stigmatize another's faults from without can only shut him up in himself.

At this turning – point in contemporary history, it becomes more urgent than ever before for us all to consider the essence of our common life, and to make the adaptations that need to be made. By its very nature every community life is turned towards both God and men. If it encouraged purity of life alone, it would be in danger of dying a slow death. It calls for the capacity to adapt to renewals. Those living in community use the freedom of their situation to best advantage when they are an hour ahead by the clock of human societies and that of the Church. Being too far ahead would do nobody any good. But lagging behind would destroy the momentum of a life given for others.

Today more than ever, when it is charged with the life-force proper to it, when it is filled with the freshness of brotherly love which is its distinctive feature, community life is like yeast at work in the dough. It can raise mountains of apathy, and bring to men an irreplaceable quality of the presence of Christ.

REMAINING IN CONTEMPLATIVE
WAITING UPON GOD

Remaining in Contemplative Waiting Upon God

WAITING AND THE PROVISIONAL

How often, when we are together in church for common prayer, I am in a state of amazement! These men, my brothers, my lifelong companions, remain faithful in their contemplative waiting upon God. They wait in God's presence without seeing, without knowing what the response to their waiting will be. I marvel at the earnestness of these men, their faithfulness, and the joy that dominates their inner combat.

It is so true that during our whole lives as Christians we are always in a state of waiting. Since Abraham, the first believer, and with all who come after him, we are waiting for God, for his justice, and for the event which will come from him. For anyone who has stopped waiting, anyone who has settled down in himself, his privileges or his rights, a whole dimension of faith has shrivelled away.

To realize this means realizing as well that we are living in a state that is always provisional. Provisional has the same root as provide. Provide the measures necessary until another set of circumstances arises.

At Taizé, we are convinced that all that constitutes our particular family spirit, for example our Rule and our liturgical prayer, will perhaps disappear one day. Our

67

liturgy, that powerful means of moulding us into one communion of faith, and our Rule, are instruments which make it possible for us to live in the hope of unity. In some respects are they not simply provisional elements, bound to disappear the day when all Christians are once again visibly in communion?

Anyone who lives in the provisional sees his progress constantly reinvigorated, for the supreme danger would be to become self–sufficient, to fasten the strap round our treasure trove, a liturgy for instance, and thus set up for centuries to come structures which would very quickly turn into factors producing isolation.

Can we not see in Christian history so many institutions which, in an endeavour to endure through the ages, have lost the provisional character of their beginnings? The Christian vision of their adherents becomes narrower and narrower. They can only survive by digging in behind protective barriers.

There is no reconciliation without mutual sacrifices. On the day when visible communion between Christians becomes a reality, we will have to die to ourselves, and sometimes die to what was most characteristic of the family we used to live with at a certain time and place.

What will have to disappear are the characteristics peculiar to the family, and certainly not the elements common to all. For Christian couples as for ourselves, the basis of our vocation is unalterable, particularly the vows and promises. These cannot be called into question because they constitute not only the way in which we commit ourselves to follow Christ, but the framework which keeps us together as one family.

It must be said that only someone with a sense of continuity can benefit from the dynamic of the provisional. Enthusiasm, fervour, is a positive force, but it is by no means enough. It burns itself out and vanishes if it does not transmit its momentum to another force, deeper and less perceptible, which enables us to keep on going our whole life long. It is indispensable to ensure continuity, for times of enthusiasm alternate with periods of lifelessness, arid deserts.

So it is with regularity in prayer. To complain about the faithfulness necessary would be, in fact, to complain about oneself; one day, the regularity and the continuity will be the springboard for a new leap forward.

Both are needed: enthusiasm in the perspective of the provisional, and continuity in the perspective of hope.

PEOPLE OF PEACE

The ecumenical vocation is assuredly ordeal by fire, a combat which requires complete self – mastery. In the face of tensions, only contemplative waiting allows us to preserve that inner vitality which comes from our love for Christ and for his Body, the Church. In order not to get bogged down in useless discussions or justifications which satisfy nobody, and above all to keep alive a vision of the needs of contemporary society, it is vital for our wills to be tempered in the wellsprings of contemplation.

No one who does not quench his thirst there can remain serene in the face of attitudes which must be analyzed if they are not to bring us to a dead halt in our progress, attitudes which otherwise may well sap our vital energies.

There are the pressures to conform in various ways, and the resistances to all the changes which unity will require. There are the Church leaders who call themselves ecumenists, yet keep postponing the day of visible communion so that, in fact, they exclude its possibility. There is also the small – mindedness of people, by no means uncultured, who seem to have an irresistible need to put labels on their neighbours, twisting the meaning of their words in an attempt to stifle all dialogue. There is incomprehensible jealousy, an open sore in the People of God. Jealousy seeks compensation by neutralizing the dynamism of new ventures.

Was it not Bernanos who wrote that all adventures of the spirit are a *via crucis?*

Every road to reconciliation involves a continual dying to self. None of those who travel this road can avoid trials and sufferings, even if they are sometimes tempted to run away from them.

To every Christian community God gives a place of peace and joy where we can rest in him alone, and pass through both trials and days of gladness. Conversing with

God stimulates fervour. It sets us in the communion of all the saints, alive or departed. It prepares and nourishes our communication with others by making us reflect God as bearers of his peace.

When, with two of my brothers, I met Pope John XXIII for the last time, he explained to us how he came to his decisions in very simple prayer, in serenity, in conversation with God. 'I have a dialogue with God,' he said, adding immediately: 'Oh! very humbly. Oh! quite simply.'

When someone converses with God, he does not expect any extraordinary illuminations. He knows that the most important thing, for himself and for others, is peace. Anyone who listens, by day or through the long watches of the night, is given the answer: peace!

Inner peace! Not a peace uttered by the lips while within there is war. Not a peace acquired once and for all, for there is still the burden of our own self and the incompletely healed wounds in which all kinds of feelings are still festering — bitterness, the passions seething in our flesh, illusions of impossible love or the discontent of love disappointed. All this weighs us down and tears us apart, but the peace of Christ is able to reach into the depths, even into the deepest wounds of our being.

Peace is not inner passivity nor escape from our neighbour. The peace of Christ has nothing in common with that insipid tranquillity in which the horizon contracts more and more, and in the end crushes the victim it encloses.

No peace is possible if we forget our neighbour. Every day the same question rings out: 'What have you done with your brother?' A peace which does not lead to communication and brotherly communion is nothing but illusion. The man who is at peace with himself is led to his neighbour. He inspires reconciliation and peace among those who are divided.

The peace of Christ needs time to mature, for it must heal the wounds of trials and sufferings. But now they no longer overflow; they are kept within oneself, and their hidden presence releases vital energy.

By his inner harmony with God, a man of peace is already an anticipation of unity. He carries others along with him.

At Taizé we have discovered that commitment to the chastity of celibacy is intimately linked up with contemplative waiting on God. How else could this sign of an exclusive love for God be fully authentic?

When I master my body and keep it in subjection,[9] controlling it by watching, praying and working, it is solely for love of Jesus Christ. No other is able to sustain an undertaking of this kind.

In refusing monasticism, the Reformation undermined celibacy as well. It is surprising to discover that for centuries the entire Reformation joined in a conspiracy of silence around the Scriptural texts concerning celibacy. It was seen as justified only in exceptional cases, as a means of ensuring greater availability. But the motive force behind chastity, the expectation of Christ's return, celibacy as a sign of the coming Kingdom, all that disappeared from the thinking of the Reformation.

When Luther broke his monastic vows, not only life in community, but also the vocation and the commitment to celibacy, almost completely disappeared from Protestantism. When we want to attack a position we are tempted to caricature it: cases of immorality were generalized, and the call of the Gospel disqualified for centuries.

Today men committed in a community or in the priesthood try to discover in our life at Taizé a confirmation of their call to celibacy, since we were under no obligation to look in that direction. The basis for any solidarity which exists lies in our common endeavour to live authentically this mysterious call of Christ.

God designates ambassadors of Christ those who, despite their human limitations, respond with the yes and amen of a faithful heart.

Celibacy opens our ecumenical vision to incomparable dimensions. Through it we want to be men whose lives are so completely focused on the hope of God that they wish to keep nothing back for themselves. This involves an exercise in openness to the universal, a truly ecumenical openness which allows us, with hearts ready and waiting, to take on all the concerns of our neighbour, all that comes our way.

To anyone who has no family of his own, God gives a heart and a mind able to love every family, human or spiritual. Anyone whose arms, for Christ's sake and the Gospel's, are open to all, enclosing no one person, is able to live the demands of ecumenicity and so understand every human situation. Any seeker after God who makes Christ his first love, finds it possible to assure a hidden presence of Christ among people who cannot believe.

What is expressed here represents a discovery we have made at Taizé, and might appear to exclude marriage. But it cannot be repeated too often: the vocation to celibacy can only enhance the value of the vocation to marriage. A life of fidelity to the marriage bond can likewise only be lived in waiting on God.

The community of marriage contains in miniature so many ecclesial values! Some Church fathers called it a 'little Church.' Those who struggle, day after day, to remain faithful in an indissoluble unity are bearers of ecumenicity in their own right.

INTIMACY AND SOLITUDE

A good part of people's energy is consumed in attempting to live lives of complete emotional fulfilment. Man hungers for intimacy with other human beings. And his passionate quest drives him to desire human relationships with nothing held back, communication with no reservations. Intimacy appears to be a goal without which no earthly happiness is possible, and its image is alluring as no other.

Any self – examination leads to the conclusion that every intimate relationship, even between the most united partners, inevitably has its limitations. Beyond them, we are alone. Anyone who refuses to accept this natural order of things will, as a result of his refusal, find himself in revolt.

Accepting our fundamental alone – ness sets us on the road to peace, and allows the Christian to discover a previously unknown dimension of his relationship with God. Acceptance of this portion of loneliness, a condition of every human life, fosters intimacy with Him who rescues us from the overwhelming solitude of the man alone with himself.

To say to Christ 'I love you' leads us to embody our intention in a gesture or an action, if it is not to remain mere words. If we are willing, for Christ's sake, to fight out our inner combats to the very end, even though we may, for the time being, be wounded to the quick, then intimacy with Him will fill our solitudes; from then on someone will be there.

Intimacy with Him will be communion and will sustain a faith able to move mountains.

CONTEMPLATIVE WAITING

The contemplative life is not an existence hovering between heaven and earth, in ecstasy or illumination. It begins when in humility we come closer to God and to our neighbour. It is always stamped with the seal of a practical mind.

It lays down one condition: keep inner silence at all times. There are ways of attaining this, at work or when alone: frequently invoking the name of Jesus, saying or singing a Psalm you know by heart, or making the simple gesture of the sign of the cross.

It is also a certain way of looking at one's neighbour, a vision transfigured by reconciliation. Anyone who is continually faced with a variety of different individuals finds refreshment in these children of God; fatigue itself is swept away when they are accepted with an attentiveness constantly renewed at the wellsprings of contemplation.

Contemplative waiting upon God leads us to the acceptances necessary each day: acceptance of our state of life, our growing older, acceptance of opportunities lost. Regret itself is transformed into a dynamic act, repentance, which stimulates our advance.

In *Thomas Gordeyev*, Gorki tells how on the Volga ice destroyed Ignatius' boat. A miser who watched every rouble, he accepted the loss instantly. He knew regret would be useless, and already he felt reassured and encouraged by the thought of the new boat he was going to build.

In regret the inner self disintegrates. Far from being stimulated, a man's spirit becomes sterile when it keeps on reconstructing a situation that is past and gone, giving itself over to fruitless brooding.

Some people have had a childhood that encourages unconscious remorse. We would all like to begin over again and do better. But is there anything we do really well? We live and work in the realm of the approximate. Regret sterilizes the impulse to create. Regret debilitates.

If we are granted a time of certainty, security and sure ground, it is when we are gathered together in contemplative waiting on God. Then, everything is possible once more. Even the salt recovers its savour; what was insipid has value again.

In contemplative waiting all our innate pessimism dissolves, even if this pessimism is rooted in what we actually see in society or in ourselves.

There are so many reasons for pessimism in the world today. There are the masses of people, increasing day by day, without any sense of God, and the Christian societies which are turned in upon themselves. There is the prospect of seeing, twenty years from now, four thousand million human beings living in deprivation, while one thousand million live in plenty. There is the huge wave slowly breaking over us: a technological civilization encapsulating man and submerging him in its totality.

There are also inner grounds for discouragement: the combat we live day after day, and the old self that refuses to submit – the pride of life, the stubborn will which persists in taking no account of its neighbour, the weight of fatigue. So many reasons in life for pessimism.

In contemplative waiting upon God everything becomes desirable again. Pessimism is watered down and yields to the optimism of faith. Then and only then is it possible to consider what is coming towards us and to welcome the events of the present time, to run towards our neighbour, to make a new start, to go forward. It is only in contemplative waiting upon God that we can find new momentum.

Wait!

Wait for the dawning of a life, when God will gather us into his arms for ever.

Wait for God to act, in ourselves and in others.

Wait for a communion within the People of God which will spark a communion among all people.

Wait for the springtime of the Church.

Wait, in spite of everything, for the spirit of mercy, for love which is not a consuming fire is not charity, and without charity we would be professing ecumenism without hope.

God is preparing for us a new Pentecost which will set every one of us ablaze with the fire of his love. Our part is to run and meet the event which will upset all our human calculations and bring life to our dry bones.

Run towards, not away!

Run to meet mankind's tomorrow, a technological civilization fully charged with potential for human development.

Run to meet all who cannot believe, and to struggle alongside the most exploited.

Run to support a rebirth of the People of God, asking and imploring them, in season and out of season, to come together, and so to raise up in the world of men an unmistakable sign of our brotherly love.

78

Run towards a Christian community wearied by its long journeyings, and do everything possible to keep the ecumenical wave from falling back.

NOTES

1. Psalm 22.8
2. Matthew 21.31
3. Acts 3.6
4. Galatians 6.2
5. Weimarer Ausgabe, Vol. II, p 605
6. Instructions of Pope Adrian VI to the Nuncio F. Chieregati in Karl MIRBT, *Quellen zur Geschichte des Papsttums und des romischen Katholizismus*, 5th ed., Tubingen 1934, p 261
7. PETER THE VENERABLE, *Sermon sur la louange du Sépulcre du Seigneur*, (Revue Bénédictine) 1954, p 242
8. SAINT BERNARD, *Letter 254*, Patrologie latine, Vol. 182, p 461
9. 1 Corinthians 9.27